PATRICK H. PERRINE

Fueling the Fire

Nurturing Resilience and Preventing Burnout in Entrepreneurship

amazon kindle

DEDICATION

To every entrepreneur who courageously stakes their all on the altar of dreams, this book is for you. It is for the tireless visionaries who brave the unpredictable seas of entrepreneurship, those undeterred by the formidable waves of challenges. It is for the dreamers who dare to ignite the spark of an idea, and the warriors who fan that spark into a flame.

- Patrick H. Perrine

"Success is not final, failure is not fatal: It is the courage to continue that counts."

- WINSTON CHURCHILL

Contents

Preface

My journey from being a paperboy in Minnesota to becoming a globally recognized entrepreneur has been an eventful ride, full of grit, determination, and resilience. But it has not been without its challenges. Burnout is a very real part of entrepreneurship, one that I have faced and overcome more than once. It is a silent predator that can consume you if you let it. My personal experiences and encounters with burnout form the backbone of this book, "Fueling the Fire."

As you journey through these pages, you will encounter stories of entrepreneurs who have dared to face the fire of burnout and have emerged stronger. You'll discover strategies to nurture your resilience and ways to guard yourself against the burnout that threatens so many of us in this high-stakes world.

This book is more than just a manual on managing burnout. It's an invitation to learn from our shared experiences, to fuel your drive, and to align your work with your values. It is my hope that "Fueling the Fire" will serve as a beacon to you, lighting your path through the demanding landscape of entrepreneurship, and helping you create your own legacy of success.

- Patrick H. Perrine

1

The Eye of the Storm: Confronting the Ghost of Burnout

E mbarking on the journey of entrepreneurship is akin to setting sail on an ocean of dreams. You're a beacon of passion and resolve, navigating through the endless horizon of possibility, fuelled by your will to sculpt the abstract into tangible reality. Yet, amidst the thrills of this voyage, a silent specter lurks beneath the waves: the phantom of burnout. Our first chapter pulls back the curtain on this subtle intruder, illuminating the nuances of burnout, its toll on entrepreneurs, and the imperative of preemptive measures.

In the Grip of Burnout: Burnout doesn't simply mean being wearied or anxious. It is a crippling trifecta of emotional, mental, and physical fatigue, born out of extended engagement with relentless stressors. The entrepreneurial life, with its distinctive hurdles and pressures—tight deadlines, funding pursuits, team management, and constant uncertainties—can nurture this oppressive fatigue, eroding your vitality bit by bit.

Burnout is a shapeshifter, manifesting uniquely in each of

us. However, its tell-tale signs are universal: a ceaseless weariness, waning motivation, escalating cynicism, irritability, and physical signs like headaches or insomnia. Heeding these red flags is vital. Letting burnout remain unnoticed can precipitate severe repercussions for your mental, emotional, and physical wellbeing.

On the Battlefield of Startup Founders: As a founder, you wrestle with unique hurdles that can fan the flames of burnout. The formidable pressure to triumph, donning multiple roles, and the constant need for swift adaptation make the entrepreneurial terrain a battlefield. Scarce resources, financial limitations, and the burden of responsibility can compound this stress.

The entrepreneurial realm thrives on change. Market conditions, customer demands, industry trends shift swiftly and relentlessly, demanding founders to remain ever-agile and adaptable. This state of constant flux, along with the balancing act of multiple roles, can usher in an overwhelming sense of pressure, fueling burnout.

The pursuit of lofty goals, while laudable, can also become a double-edged sword. The relentless chase of disruptive innovation and extraordinary growth, without pausing to gauge its impact on your wellbeing, can become a one-way ticket to burnout.

The Echoes of Burnout: Burnout can cast long shadows over your wellbeing and your startup's growth. It drains your life force, leaving your motivation, creativity, and productivity parched. This depletion can cloud your decision-making abilities, diminishing your effectiveness.

Moreover, burnout can strain your interpersonal relationships. Persistent fatigue and irritability can spark conflicts with colleagues, partners, and loved ones, causing your startup's morale and productivity to plummet.

Beyond the immediate impact, burnout can lay the groundwork for chronic physical and mental health issues. The constant stress can compromise your immune system and contribute to conditions like cardiovascular disease and metabolic disorders. Burnout's toll on mental health can trigger anxiety, depression, and other disorders, impeding your capacity to flourish as an entrepreneur.

By deciphering the code of burnout, you're already taking the first step towards barricading it. Recognizing the symptoms, acknowledging the unique challenges of being a founder, and comprehending the fallout of burnout sets the stage for nurturing resilience and wellbeing.

The chapters ahead will traverse through practical strategies to avert burnout, fostering resilience and entrepreneurial growth. We'll journey through self-care, crafting a support system, managing time, setting boundaries, cultivating adaptability, nurturing a healthy work culture, and finding joy in your entrepreneurial endeavors.

Preventing burnout isn't about working harder or bracing against the challenges. It demands a holistic approach, harmonizing self-awareness, self-care, and a nurturing environment. Implementing these strategies lays the foundation for sustainable success.

It's crucial to remember that burnout isn't an inevitable pitstop on your entrepreneurial journey. Prioritize your wellbeing and adopt proactive measures to keep burnout at bay. Your wellbeing is your most valuable asset, indispensable for the lasting success of your startup.

As we journey together through these chapters, I urge you to embrace each lesson with an open heart and the readiness to apply the strategies that resonate with you. Remember, warding off burnout is a continuous endeavor, necessitating commitment, introspection, and an adaptability to change when needed.

In this book, we'll offer guidance, practical exercises, and real-life examples to aid you in your quest to avert burnout and flourish as an entrepreneur. By nurturing your resilience and wellbeing, you can stoke the embers of your passion, creativity, and entrepreneurial spirit, ensuring a fulfilling and sustainable entrepreneurial voyage.

Case Study: The Iron Man Meltdown: Elon Musk's Battle with Burnout

Elon Musk, the powerhouse behind Tesla and SpaceX, is a paragon of entrepreneurial resilience. He's an emblem of innovation, defying odds to revolutionize industries. Yet, in 2018, the world got a glimpse of the price Musk was paying when he openly admitted to his struggles with burnout.

In the midst of an exceptionally grueling time, Musk tweeted, "There are way easier places to work, but nobody ever changed the world on 40 hours a week." In a New York Times interview, Musk further shared the toll his work was taking on his personal life and health. During this period, Tesla was in the throes of executing an ambitious production ramp-up for the Model 3. Musk was working up to 120 hours a week, rarely seeing his family, and his physical health was deteriorating.

Musk's schedule was so extreme that he barely had time to go home to shower. He kept a sleeping bag in a conference room adjacent to Tesla's production line. This punishing work routine, while it facilitated Tesla's short-term goals, was not sustainable in the long run. Elon Musk, the high-octane innovator, was burning out.

The repercussions were not confined to Musk's health. His exhaustion likely contributed to a few public relations issues and erratic behavior, such as suddenly announcing a plan to take Tesla private, which resulted in a significant investigation by the SEC.

Musk's burnout was a wake-up call. After this period, Musk started to make changes. Tesla began hiring more staff to alleviate the load and provide Musk some respite. While Musk still maintains an extraordinarily demanding schedule, he has admitted the importance of having more balance, stating in an Axios interview that 80-90 hours per week are more sustainable.

Elon Musk's experience underscores the reality that even the most prodigious entrepreneurs aren't immune to burnout. It underscores the crucial lesson that perpetually pushing the limits of endurance isn't a sustainable strategy for entrepreneurial success. Prioritizing wellbeing and balance isn't merely essential for personal health; it's integral for the long-term health and success of the businesses entrepreneurs are trying to build.

Elon Musk's burnout journey serves as a potent reminder of the importance of recognizing and addressing burnout. Even in the storm of entrepreneurial demands, taking care of one's health should never take the backseat. As we delve deeper into this book, let Musk's experience guide us in the journey towards preventing burnout, fostering resilience, and cultivating sustainable success in entrepreneurship.

A Personal Pause: Reflecting on Our Own Limits

As we take a moment to breathe in the wake of Musk's daunting experience with burnout, I invite you to pause and engage in a personal reflection. This reflection is not merely a passive pause; it is a purposeful pause. It's an opportunity for you to take stock of your current state of being, and to hone in on the whispers of burnout that might be lingering in the shadows.

In this personal pause, ask yourself:

- **What are my personal warning signs of burnout?** Consider the unique ways in which stress manifests for you. It might be irritability, constant fatigue, or a nagging feeling of disillusionment. Recognizing these early signals can be your first line of defense against burnout.
- **What boundaries have I set for myself?** Reflect on the boundaries that you've drawn for your well-being. Are they firm? Or do they often get blurred in the heat of pressing deadlines and burgeoning responsibilities?
- **Am I nurturing my holistic well-being?** Remember, resilience is not just about mental strength but involves nurturing your physical, emotional, and spiritual well-being too. Consider the last time you took a step back to simply rejuvenate and realign with your purpose.
- **What lessons can I draw from Musk's narrative?** Musk's story is not just a tale of caution but also one of resilience and recovery. It brings to the fore the importance of adaptability and the courage to pivot when necessary

for your well-being. What insights from Musk's journey resonate with you?

As you mull over these questions, allow yourself to acknowledge and validate your feelings and experiences without judgment. This moment of reflection can be your sacred space of honesty and self-compassion, a cornerstone in building resilience against burnout.

Remember, the entrepreneurial journey is not a sprint; it's a marathon. Nurturing your well-being isn't a luxury; it's a necessity, integral to fostering the endurance needed for the long haul. As you stand on the brink of this deep exploration into preventing burnout, carry with you the awareness and insights garnered in this personal pause. It can serve as your compass, guiding you to traverse the challenging yet rewarding landscape of entrepreneurship with resilience, grace, and sustainable vigor.

In our next chapter, we'll delve into the cornerstone of burnout prevention: self-care. We'll traverse through an array of self-care practices and techniques to help you rejuvenate, strike a balance, and foster resilience. Join me as we unfold the transformative power of self-care on your entrepreneurial journey.

2

Igniting Vitality: The Transformative Role of Self-Care in Forestalling Burnout

In the thrilling symphony of entrepreneurship, each note counts, each pause matters, and in this intricate composition, the one wielding the baton - the entrepreneur - is pivotal. This chapter breathes life into the melody of self-care. It opens up the narrative of self-care not as an afterthought, but as a potent strategy to fortify you, the conductor, against the omnipresent threat of burnout. As you sow the seeds of your startup dream, it is vital to remember that nurturing your own well-being is the lifeline that sustains your entrepreneurial vitality.

Decoding Self-Care: In an entrepreneurial world often governed by relentless pursuit and dogged determination, self-care could mistakenly be perceived as self-indulgence or a distraction. But let's shed light on its true essence. Self-care is an intentional, pro-active commitment to replenishing your physical, mental, and emotional reserves. It's the conscious choice of paving the path for a more fulfilled and healthier you, enabling you to meet your goals with vigor and resilience.

Your Body, Your Temple: The axis of your entrepreneurial voyage is your physical health, the temple that houses your dreams, aspirations, and abilities. The entrepreneurial marathon can sometimes lead to neglect of this temple, potentially triggering fatigue, productivity drop, and increased vulnerability to illness. Fortify this foundation by embracing regular exercise, nourishing your body with a balanced diet, and immersing yourself in the restorative embrace of restful sleep.

Rest, Relax, Recharge: Every symphony requires pauses to make the melody resonate, and so does the rhythm of entrepreneurship. Rest and relaxation are the restorative pauses that infuse harmony into your busy cadence. Intersperse your daily symphony with refreshing breaks, engage in leisure activities that bring you joy, and immerse in hobbies that serve as your sanctuaries. These replenishing islands will serve as your energizing lifeboats in the turbulent sea of entrepreneurial challenges.

Mindfulness: The tumultuous journey of entrepreneurship brings along a heavy cargo of stress. However, mindfulness can light the way through the storm, allowing you to navigate with ease and resilience. Infuse mindfulness into your work approach, bringing awareness to your thoughts, feelings, and physical sensations. Techniques such as deep breathing, meditation, and journaling can anchor you in calmness and clarity, enabling you to respond, rather than react, to stress.

Embrace the Emotional Voyage: The journey of entrepreneurship is an emotional voyage, fraught with highs and lows. As you navigate these turbulent waters, don't forget to drop the anchor of emotional well-being. It's crucial to harness emotional intelligence, manage emotions effectively, and seek a supportive hand when waves are high. Cultivate healthy coping mechanisms, be it confiding in loved ones, seeking professional help, or joining entrepreneurial support groups.

Designing Your Self-Care Blueprint: To make self-care a sustainable practice, weave it into your daily routine, creating a customized self-care blueprint that caters to your unique needs and preferences. This could mean carving out time for exercise, setting a sleep schedule, practicing daily mindfulness, or scheduling joy-inducing activities. With self-care as a priority, you're not just preserving your well-being, but fortifying yourself to sail through your entrepreneurial journey with vigor and resilience.

Self-care is not a luxury, it's an entrepreneurial imperative. Prioritizing your physical, mental, and emotional well-being is a powerful strategy for forestalling burnout and nurturing long-term success. By appreciating the transformative role of self-care, embracing mindfulness, and creating a tailored self-care routine, you're stoking the flames of resilience, empowering yourself to stand tall amidst entrepreneurial challenges.

Case Study: The Highs and Lows of Leadership: Arianna Huffington's Journey Towards Work-Life Balance

Arianna Huffington, co-founder of The Huffington Post and founder of Thrive Global, is an iconic entrepreneur recognized worldwide. Despite her success, Arianna's journey has not been smooth-sailing. She experienced firsthand the harsh consequences of ignoring self-care in her entrepreneurial pursuits, ultimately leading to a personal health crisis that served as a wake-up call.

In 2007, at the height of her career, Arianna fainted from exhaustion in her office, suffering a broken cheekbone and a nasty gash over her eye. The incident served as a stern reminder of the toll that relentless hustle, inadequate sleep, and a lack of self-care could exert on one's health. "This is not a sustainable way of working," she reflected. The incident marked a turning point, and Arianna embarked on a quest to redefine success by prioritizing well-being.

Arianna began to incorporate self-care into her routine, investing time in sleep, meditation, and physical exercise. She recognized that she was not alone in her struggle; many entrepreneurs were caught up in the delusion that burnout was the price for achievement. Determined to challenge this mindset, Arianna launched Thrive Global in 2016, a platform dedicated to promoting well-being and productivity, helping others understand the transformative role of self-care in preventing burnout.

Today, Arianna Huffington is not only a celebrated entrepreneur but also an advocate for work-life balance, self-care, and mental health. Her journey underscores the importance of rest, relaxation, and self-care in preserving health and fostering sustainable success. Her example serves as a powerful reminder that the choice to invest in one's well-being is not just a personal decision, but a business one.

In Arianna's words, "The way we're working isn't working." Through her actions, she encourages entrepreneurs to break free from the traditional, often harmful, notions of success. She demonstrates the profound impact of prioritizing self-care in our lives, empowering us to become more resilient, focused, and effective leaders.

As we contemplate Arianna's story, let's remember the significance of taking care of our physical, mental, and emotional health. Self-care is not a distraction from our goals but the fuel that allows us to pursue them with vitality and resilience. Like Arianna, let's redefine success, viewing it not just in terms of professional accomplishments but also personal well-being and satisfaction. In doing so, we ensure not only the success of our ventures but also our lasting health and happiness.

A Personal Pause: Reflecting on the Birth of My Self-Care Journey

As we draw this chapter to a close, I find myself reflecting on the early days of my entrepreneurial journey, a time that feels both a lifetime ago and just yesterday. It was then, amidst the whirlpool of setting up a startup, that I made my first hire - an Executive Assistant named Adam. In many ways, he sowed the seeds of a philosophy that would come to guide my approach to entrepreneurship: the transformative power of self-care.

Adam, with years of experience and an intuitive understanding of the rigors of the entrepreneurial world, instilled in me a practice that has stood the test of time. He encouraged scheduling an additional 30 to 45 minutes to each lunch appointment, a buffer that allowed for a meditative pause in a day often characterized by relentless pace. Initially, it was a time to reset mentally, later morphing into a dedicated slot for physical wellness, accommodating gym sessions at least thrice a week, forging a sanctuary of rejuvenation amidst a hectic schedule.

Two decades later, the spirit of this ritual lives on, albeit in a transformed manner. The gym sessions have been replaced by tranquil walks along the beach, accompanied by my faithful dog, merging the nurturing embrace of nature with personal well-being. This time has become a crucible of preparation, a grounding ritual before facing the day's myriad challenges with a spirit rejuvenated and ready to forge ahead.

It's a practice that finds resonance in Arianna Huffington's transformative journey that we explored in this chapter. Much like how Arianna realized the need for balance, I too learned the essential role of self-care in nurturing resilience and preventing burnout. It's a lesson that transcends the boundaries of professional life, seeping into the personal, helping craft a daily routine where well-being takes center stage.

As you turn the last page of this chapter, I invite you to pause and reflect. Consider the various avenues through which you might integrate self-care into your daily life, fostering a sanctuary of peace and rejuvenation, much like the one Adam helped me discover all those years ago.

As we harbor the wisdom drawn from personal experiences and the inspirational journey of Arianna, I encourage you to conceive your own self-care blueprint, one that caters to your unique needs and preferences, empowering you not just to prevent burnout but to thrive in your entrepreneurial journey with vigor and resilience.

In this reflection, I wish for you to find the courage to prioritize yourself, to acknowledge the essential role of self-care in nurturing the flames of resilience, fueling a fulfilling and successful entrepreneurial voyage.

As we embark on the chapters to follow, remember that self-care is not an indulgence but a necessity, a vital force energizing the entrepreneurial spirit, nurturing it from a fledgling spark to a roaring flame, ready to face and overcome the challenges that lie ahead with strength, grace, and unwavering resolve.

3

Building Castles of Resilience: The Impact of a Robust Support System

U nveiling the third movement of our entrepreneurial symphony, we delve into the strength and solace found in building a solid support system. The entrepreneurial journey, a thrilling orchestration of triumphs and trials, beckons for a chorus of voices that provide guidance, encouragement, and a sense of unity.

The Symphony of Support: Navigating the labyrinth of entrepreneurship might occasionally instill a sense of solitude, with the entire symphony's onus seeming to rest solely upon your shoulders. Yet, the notion of a solitary struggle is far from the truth. Crafting a robust support system empowers you to lean on others for wisdom, motivation, and emotional succor. This fellowship of supporters can shed a new light on your experiences, ensure your accountability, and provide a wellspring of insight drawn from their own odysseys.

Harmonizing Relationships: The cornerstone of a strong

support system is the cultivation of meaningful relationships. Search for those individuals who echo your entrepreneurial passion, comprehend the hurdles you encounter, and harbor an authentic desire for your success. This cadre may comprise fellow entrepreneurs, mentors, advisors, or industry cognoscenti, who can offer guidance, reveal their expertise, and act as sounding boards to your innovative inklings and apprehensions.

Creating Melodies through Networking: Networking is your conductor's baton to broaden your support system. Seize the opportunity to attend industry conclaves, join entrepreneurship-centric organizations, and partake in conferences and meetups. Such avenues enable you to harmonize with like-minded maestros, share narratives, and forge relationships that can provide solace and synergy. Seek both local and online communities where you can engage in discourse, seek advice, and receive valuable feedback from your entrepreneurial ensemble.

Mentors and Advisors: Mentors and advisors offer a veritable crescendo of invaluable guidance on your entrepreneurial path. Seek seasoned individuals who have orchestrated success in your industry or possess expertise in areas where you seek enlightenment. Mentorship, akin to a beautiful symphony, can be a mutually enriching relationship that nurtures growth and fosters learning.

Emotional Cadence with Friends and Family: The rhythm of your personal life—your friends and family—plays an instrumental role in forestalling burnout. Share your entrepreneurial journey with your loved ones and seek their understanding and support. Their emotional backing, their faith in your abilities, and their encouragement can be the most powerful melody to inspire resilience.

Professional Support: Therapists, Coaches, and Support Groups: At times, you might need to extend your support network beyond immediate connections. Professional resources like therapists, coaches, or support groups can offer a safe haven to explore your feelings, overcome challenges, and devise strategies to prevent burnout. This professional chorus can provide invaluable insights, tools, and coping strategies to enrich your well-being.

Conducting Reciprocal Relationships: Building a support system isn't merely about receiving support—it's also about offering it. Engage actively within your relationships, offer assistance, and be a wellspring of encouragement. Fostering reciprocally supportive relationships orchestrates a network of individuals who comprehend the unique cadences of entrepreneurship and are committed to mutual prosperity.

The Art of Nurturing Your Support System: Crafting a support system is an ongoing performance. It demands consistent communication, active engagement, and genuine investment in others' well-being. Carve out time to connect with your support network through regular encounters, virtual check-ins, or shared endeavors. Appreciate the support you receive and reciprocate with kindness when others seek your help.

Coda: Creating a robust support system is an instrumental factor in staving off burnout. Surrounding yourself with individuals who understand and support your entrepreneurial voyage provides guidance, encouragement, and a sense of belonging. From swapping tales with fellow entrepreneurs to seeking wisdom from mentors and advisors, every connection within your support system contributes to your resilience and well-being. Remember to nurture these bonds and reciprocate the support, thereby weaving a network of mutual sustenance.

Case Study: Sailing the Entrepreneurial Seas: Richard Branson and The Power of a Support System

Sir Richard Branson, founder of the Virgin Group and a revered icon in the entrepreneurial world, is no stranger to the value of a solid support system. With more than 400 companies under the Virgin banner, Branson's extraordinary success story is not solely his own but is a testament to the power of cultivating meaningful relationships and harnessing the collective strength of a supportive network.

Throughout his entrepreneurial journey, Branson has consistently emphasized the importance of building and maintaining a robust network of supportive individuals. He attributes much of his success to the guidance, advice, and support he received from mentors, peers, and his team. His approach to business highlights how a supportive network can ignite innovation, inspire resilience, and prevent burnout.

One of the key figures in Branson's supportive network was his mother, Eve Branson. A trailblazer herself, Eve was Richard's earliest mentor, instilling in him the values of determination, resilience, and positivity. She was a constant source of emotional support and encouragement, fostering his entrepreneurial spirit from a young age.

Branson's journey was also enriched by his interactions with mentors and advisors from various industries. Freddy Laker, a fellow British aviation entrepreneur, played a crucial role in guiding Branson through the intricacies of the airline industry when he was establishing Virgin Atlantic. Branson's mentorship relationship with Laker is a classic example of how seasoned professionals' wisdom and experience can provide invaluable insights, guide decision-making, and foster learning.

Richard Branson's philosophy also extends to his team and the culture he cultivates within his businesses. His commitment to creating an environment where everyone feels heard, valued, and supported reflects the significance he places on fostering a strong support network. Branson strongly believes in the power of teamwork and the importance of nurturing a community in which everyone supports each other. "A business is simply an idea to make other people's lives better," Branson states, underscoring the emphasis he places on relationships and mutual support within his ventures.

Lastly, Branson's approach to networking is noteworthy. He doesn't view networking as a one-sided venture but sees it as an opportunity to establish mutually beneficial relationships. His enthusiastic participation in various conferences, events, and social causes underscores his belief in the power of networking in creating meaningful connections, learning from others, and identifying new opportunities.

Richard Branson's story exemplifies the instrumental role a robust support system plays in the entrepreneurial journey. The support he received from his mother, mentors like Freddy Laker, his team, and his wider network all contributed to his resilience and helped him navigate the complexities and challenges of entrepreneurship. Branson's journey serves as an inspiring reminder of the strength and solace that can be found in building a solid support system. His example reinforces the notion that an entrepreneurial journey is not a solitary endeavor but a shared voyage that can be enriched by the collective wisdom, experiences, and support of others.

A Personal Pause: The Longevity of Valuable Relationships

As I reflect upon the cradle of my own entrepreneurial journey, spanning over two decades, I find myself revisiting the proverb "birds of a feather flock together." Time has fostered reliance on a steadfast group of individuals, connections forged in the crucible of past experiences, still holding valuable and true today.

I have carried forth lessons imparted by mentors and peers, treasured tidbits of wisdom, into present encounters, sharing them with new contacts, clients, and coworkers. These little nuggets of wisdom are now passed on, continuing their journey from one individual to another, nurturing growth and fostering understanding in an ever-widening circle of influence.

Today, as I venture into new realms, building relationships through individuals who have stood by me in the past, I find myself enriched and guided by connections old and new. I realize the depth of wisdom housed in past experiences and the myriad ways in which they shape my present and guide my future.

The lessons learned and the relationships nurtured have

transformed into a guiding force, a beacon of light, illuminating the path of entrepreneurial resilience. It underlines the value of maintaining and nurturing relationships, allowing them to evolve, and realizing that even as time marches on, the learnings from the past continue to hold relevance, offering a wellspring of knowledge and a foundation of support as enduring as time itself.

As our symphonic journey continues, we will transition into a movement that addresses a pillar of entrepreneurship often overshadowed by grandeur visions and exciting innovations yet is no less vital: time management and productivity. The next chapter lays out a cadence of strategies that aid in defining priorities, setting realistic goals, and managing your workload adeptly to prevent burnout.

Equipped with the invaluable support system we cultivated in this chapter, we stand on a solid ground ready to venture into mastering the art of steering our entrepreneurial ship efficiently through the undulating waves of time. Let us forge ahead with anticipation, guided by our supportive ensemble, as we learn to harmonize our efforts with time, the most relentless yet fair judge, in the next movement of our entrepreneurial symphony.

Join us in the forthcoming chapter as we unravel the secret to marrying passion with productivity, carving out a narrative where dreams are realized through disciplined effort, where our vision is translated into reality one well-planned step at a time. Let's embark on this journey of discovery, sculpting our symphony with a renewed vigor and a blueprint for success that stands the test of time.

4

Harmonizing the Tempo: The Art of Time Management and Productivity

In this captivating chapter, we venture into a critical dimension of the entrepreneurial journey: Time Management and Productivity. A cornerstone in the framework of successful entrepreneurship, it is pivotal in averting the debilitating effects of burnout. Entrepreneurs, your time is a rare gem, and its effective management forms the bedrock of your well-being, attainment of objectives, and shielding against burnout.

The Symphony of Time Management: Time management is the deliberate art of setting your tempo and tuning your activities to the rhythm of your aspirations and values. By taking command of your time, you can curtail stress, elevate productivity, and strike a harmonious balance in your life.

Setting Priorities and Goals: To effectively conduct your time, it's vital to lay down clear priorities and goals. Begin by pinpointing the tasks and activities that resonate with your long-term vision and add the most value to your startup. Deconstruct your larger goals into smaller, manageable tasks, and allocate realistic timelines. This clarity will enable you to stay focused on your key performance pieces and avoid wasting time on less essential rehearsals.

The Crescendo of Task Management and Organization: A fundamental aspect of time management is effective task management and organization. Choose a system that harmonizes with your workflow, be it a digital project management tool, a daily planner, or a blend of methods. Fragment your tasks into actionable steps, assign timelines, and monitor your progress. Consistently review and update your task list to ensure you stay on top of your performance and stave off feeling overwhelmed.

Hitting the High Notes: The 80/20 rule, also known as the Pareto Principle, postulates that approximately 80% of your outcomes are derived from 20% of your efforts. Apply this principle to your time management by centering on tasks that strike the highest notes. Pinpoint the 20% of activities that produce the majority of your desired outcomes and prioritize them. By doing so, you can optimize your time and energy and sidestep getting entangled in less productive compositions.

Techniques of Time Management: Time blocking is an effective technique for conducting your time wisely. By designating specific time slots for diverse activities, you create a structured rhythm and boost focus. Allot dedicated time for concentrated work, meetings, creative thinking, and respite. Experiment with various time management techniques, such as the Pomodoro Technique or the Eisenhower Matrix, to find a rhythm that aligns with your work style and maximizes your productivity.

Delegation and Outsourcing: Remember that an orchestra is composed of many instruments. Delegating tasks and outsourcing certain responsibilities can liberate valuable time and cognitive energy. Identify tasks that can be transferred to team members, contractors, or virtual assistants. Concentrate on your areas of proficiency and the tasks that truly demand your attention, while empowering others to contribute their unique skills and talents to the symphony of your startup.

Avoiding Procrastination and Time Wasters: Procrastination and indulging in time wasters can substantially slow down your productivity rhythm, fostering a fertile ground for burnout. It is essential to delineate your "producing" hours clearly, where focus and output should be your sole pursuits, relegating activities like extensive social media scrolling or engaging in unproductive discussions to their designated time and place. Recognize your personal tendencies towards procrastination and develop strategies to counteract them actively. A proactive approach could involve cultivating a conducive work environment, utilizing productivity tools, and practicing disciplined use of technology. By distinguishing between productive work hours and leisure, you pave the way for a well-balanced, productive routine that eschews burnout.

Managing Workload and Avoiding Overwhelm: Among the greatest challenges for entrepreneurs is directing a heavy workload and preventing overwhelm. Segment tasks into smaller, manageable pieces, and tackle them one at a time.

Develop a knack for effective time estimation to evade over-committing yourself. Learn to say no to tasks or projects that do not strike a chord with your priorities or that exceed your capacity. Solicit support from your team or consider outsourcing certain tasks when needed. Remember, controlling your workload effectively is key to maintaining a healthy work-life rhythm and preventing burnout.

Time Management for Personal Well-being: Effective time management doesn't just pertain to work-related tasks but also involves prioritizing activities that contribute to your personal well-being. Schedule time for self-care, physical activity, hobbies, and quality time with loved ones. Prioritizing these aspects of your life will help you recharge, sustain a sense of fulfillment, and ward off burnout.

Flexibility in Time Management: While effective time management is pivotal, adapting to the changing rhythm is crucial. Entrepreneurship often requires you to pivot, respond to sudden challenges, and alter your plans accordingly. Be open to changes in tempo and prepared to modify your schedule when necessary. Embracing flexibility allows you to maintain a sense of control and mitigates stress when unexpected obstacles arise.

Periodic Evaluation and Reflection: Take a moment to evaluate and reflect on your time management practices regularly to identify areas for improvement. Dedicate time to review your accomplishments, challenges, and lessons learned. Assess whether your current strategies are performing an effective melody and make adjustments as required. This ongoing evaluation will help you refine your time management skills and optimize your productivity.

Mastering time management is a vital composition in preventing burnout as an entrepreneur. By setting priorities, organizing tasks, employing time management techniques, delegating responsibilities, and avoiding time wasters, you can optimize your productivity, maintain a healthy work-life balance, and nurture your well-being. Remember to dance with flexibility and adaptability, and regularly reflect on your time management practices to continually fine-tune your performance.

Case Study: Maintaining Momentum: Indra Nooyi and the Symphony of Time Management

Rising to become the CEO of PepsiCo and maintaining that position for 12 years is no small feat, but Indra Nooyi made it look almost effortless. However, her accomplishments didn't come without a tremendous amount of hard work and effective time management. As a leader of a multinational corporation and a mother, Nooyi's skill in harmonizing her professional and personal life is nothing short of inspirational.

Nooyi often emphasizes the importance of setting clear priorities and goals. She would commence her tenure at PepsiCo with the goal of transforming the company to meet the evolving consumer health trends. This ambitious objective was then deconstructed into smaller tasks, with set timelines and action plans. This meticulous planning allowed her to keep her focus, moving the entire organization toward the shared goal.

Effective task management and organization were pivotal in Nooyi's leadership style. To streamline her workflow and keep herself organized, Nooyi would spend the last few minutes of each day planning for the next. She would review her tasks, break them down into manageable pieces, and set clear timelines, which would keep her performance at its peak and help her avoid feeling overwhelmed.

Nooyi's application of the Pareto Principle has also been evident in her approach to leading PepsiCo. She identified the "vital few" tasks that would have the most significant impact on the company's transition towards healthier products, focusing her efforts where they would be most productive. This careful allocation of resources meant less time wasted on less impactful tasks.

Nooyi is also an advocate of the power of delegation. She believed in the strength of her team and the importance of empowering others to take on responsibilities. By assigning tasks to competent team members, she was able to free up her time for strategic decision-making and visionary thinking.

The practice of avoiding procrastination and time-wasters is also one that Nooyi credits for her effective time management. She would maintain a disciplined schedule and avoid distractions to ensure maximum productivity in her professional life.

Balancing her demanding job and personal life, Nooyi also knew when to draw the line. She advocated for the importance of controlling one's workload and avoiding overwhelm, emphasizing the importance of downtime and life beyond work.

Despite her strict time management techniques, Nooyi remained flexible and adaptable to changing circumstances. She also took time to periodically evaluate her practices, adjust her plans, and refine her strategies as needed.

Indra Nooyi's symphony of time management is a testament to how effectively managing one's time can lead to significant accomplishments and the prevention of burnout. As we explore further in our entrepreneurial journey, her example lights the path to effective time management, emphasizing the power of clear priorities, effective task management, delegation, avoiding time wasters, and maintaining work-life balance.

A Personal Pause: Patrick's Rhythm of Productivity

In my personal journey, the art of time management has been a steadfast companion. It's a relationship that blossomed early in my life, even granting me a nickname among my high school friends — they would jovially refer to my deep work sessions as "Pat Productiveness Time." (Just a small note: this nickname is reserved for those who knew me before my teenage years; hearing "Pat" from anyone else is akin to nails on a chalkboard.) These sessions were a symbol of utter focus, a time when I was "in the zone," getting things done without any distractions.

Fast forward to today, this rhythm of "Pat Productiveness Time" has not just remained but intensified and refined, weaving in a golden thread of timeliness that has come to define both my personal and professional life. It echoes a deeply ingrained belief: if I am not early, I am already late.

My unwavering dedication to timeliness stands as a testimony to the deep respect I harbor for others' time. It means meticulously planning my schedule to honor every commitment, whether that's catching up with old friends over happy hour cocktails or pitching to a VC. It means showing up prepared, always five minutes early — a clear signal that I value and respect the time of others as much as my own.

This personal philosophy has sculpted my daily rhythm into a sanctuary of productivity that balances rigor with respect for every moment. Observe how my day unfolds:

- **Morning Ritual (6:30-8:30 AM)**: A time of calm and preparation, cherishing the serene morning hours while staying disconnected from the tech world, paving the way for a day spent respecting every moment's worth.
- **Plan the Day (8:30-9:00 AM)**: I set the stage for a day of timeliness, reviewing and realigning my day's schedule.
- **Pat Productiveness Time (9:00 AM - 4:00 PM, Mondays, Tuesdays and Thursdays)**: I delve into my tasks in 90 to 120-minute increments of focused time, reserving all day **Wednesdays** for *"White Board Wednesdays,"* a day for intense focus on substantial projects or for brainstorming sessions, channeling a practice cultivated at the Seamless IoT Accelerator from one of my engineering partners.
- **Designated Meeting Slots**: It is here where my reverence for time truly shines. I offer 15-minute meeting slots, but only at designated times throughout the week to ensure uninterrupted productivity. These slots are available:
  Mondays: 10:00 AM to 12:00 PM
  Tuesdays: 10:00 AM to 12:00 PM and 1:30 PM to 3:00 PM
  Thursdays: 11:00 AM to 12:30 PM

While these slots are firm, showcasing my respect for both my time and that of others, I maintain a level of flexibility, especially when collaborating with my global team members in locations like India, China, South Africa, or Romania, accommodating the rare meeting outside these windows to foster a harmonious global team dynamic.

- **Lunchtime**: A moment to nourish myself or to find rejuvenation through a walk with my dog, balancing productivity with personal well-being.
- **Evening Wind Down (6:00-6:30 PM to 8:30 PM)**: After winding down my work activities by around 6-6:30 PM, it's time for dinner, with a strict rule of no tech engagement post 8:30 PM, respecting the necessity for personal downtime and rejuvenation.
- **Friday: The Catch-All Day**: This day serves as a buffer to accomplish any P0 tasks that remained unattended during the week. Around once a month, I indulge in an extended "Adult Lunch Fridays," starting from noon and lasting until it naturally concludes, usually involving cocktails with 2-3 friends as a splendid wrap to a productive week.

Reflecting on this finely tuned dance of productivity and timeliness, it's evident that being organized is not about rigidity. It is about orchestrating a rhythm that honors work commitments while carving out spaces for leisure and personal preferences, fostering a culture where punctuality is not just respected but celebrated as a shared language of value and regard, nurturing fulfillment in both personal and professional spheres.

As we advance to the next movement, we explore the potent act of setting boundaries and articulating "no" to safeguard from burnout. Journey with me as we delve deeper into crafting strategies that prioritize well-being in the entrepreneurial odyssey.

5

The Art of Drawing Lines: Setting Boundaries and Saying No

I n this insightful chapter, we take a decisive leap into a critical component of your entrepreneurial journey - setting boundaries and asserting the power of saying no. As you carve out your niche as an entrepreneur, establishing robust boundaries serves as a protective shield, safeguarding your well-being, ensuring work-life harmony, and maintaining the reservoir of your energy and focus.

Recognizing the Necessity of Boundaries: Boundaries are the unseen parameters that govern your interaction with your work, your team, and the wider world of entrepreneurship. They serve as the firewall protecting your precious time, energy, and personal well-being. Formulating clear boundaries enables you to uphold your needs, exercise control over your itinerary, and prevent the encroachment of overwhelming demands.

Deciphering Your Boundaries: Embark on an introspective journey, reflecting on your core values, priorities, and personal thresholds. Identify the aspects of your professional and personal life that carry significant weight for you and pinpoint where you stand most susceptible to burnout. The gained self-awareness will serve as a compass in determining the boundaries you must set - be it working hours, your availability for meetings, personal time, or the type of tasks you undertake.

Articulating Expectations Clearly: Transparency in communication forms the bedrock of effective boundary-setting. Ensure your team, clients, and stakeholders are apprised of your boundaries - your working hours, preferred communication channels, and how you manage requests that fall outside these lines. Establishing expectations at the onset helps align everyone's understanding, circumventing potential conflicts or misunderstandings.

Upholding Self-Care and Well-being: Boundaries are not just barricades but signposts, guiding you towards prioritizing your self-care and overall well-being. This involves carving out time for rest, relaxation, physical exercise, and personal pursuits that invigorate and revitalize you. By prioritizing your well-being, you bring your best self to the forefront of your work, effectively thwarting burnout.

Mastering the Art of Saying No: Asserting 'no' is a crucial facet of maintaining boundaries and staving off burnout. Turning down opportunities or requests may be daunting, particularly when your entrepreneurial spirit is ablaze with ambition. However, developing the aptitude to say no safeguards your time, energy, and resources, aligning them with your goals and values. Assert your decision with tact and respect, offering alternative solutions where possible.

Handling Workload and Prioritization: Effectively upholding boundaries involves judicious workload management and task prioritization. Evaluate each task for its relevance and urgency, determining its alignment with your goals and priorities. Embrace delegation where appropriate, and concentrate your efforts on high-value activities that significantly impact your startup's success. Remember, effective prioritization allows you to create meaningful impact with lesser strain.

Carving Out Technological Boundaries: The omnipresence of technology can blur the delineation between work and personal life. Establish constraints on your technology use to prevent it from infringing on your personal time and contributing to burnout. Allot specific slots for checking emails, limit the influx of notifications, and create technology-free zones or time frames to foster disconnection and focus.

Maintaining Client Expectations: Client relationships can occasionally turn demanding, sowing the seeds of potential burnout. Clearly outline your boundaries and working conditions to clients at the inception of the relationship. Set expectations around response times, availability, and deliverables. Familiarize clients with your work ethos and provide alternate contact points for pressing matters during non-working hours.

Re-evaluating and Modifying Boundaries: Conduct periodic evaluations of your boundaries to ensure they continue to serve you effectively. As your entrepreneurial journey evolves, so may the boundaries to accommodate new challenges or opportunities. Reflect on the efficacy of your boundaries, making necessary amendments to maintain work-life harmony and evade burnout.

Setting boundaries and learning to say no are not mere options, but imperatives for averting burnout as an entrepreneur. These form the sturdy framework supporting a healthy work-life equilibrium, enabling you to sustain your zeal while preventing the harmful consequences of burnout. Remember, setting boundaries is not an act of selfishness; it's a move of self-preservation. By cherishing your needs and priorities, you can be at your best in both your work and personal life. Assert your boundaries with confidence and grace, and stand firm in upholding them. As you continue to define and maintain these boundaries, you pave the way for a healthier and more sustainable entrepreneurial journey.

Case Study: Sheryl Sandberg's Mastery of Boundaries and the Power of No

Sheryl Sandberg, the Chief Operating Officer of Facebook and founder of LeanIn.Org, has crafted a harmonious symphony between her high-stakes career and personal life. She has masterfully shown that even amidst the hustle of the Silicon Valley, it's possible to establish sturdy boundaries that guard personal well-being and familial bonds.

One of the most influential women in technology, Sandberg has made it a point to draw the line clearly between her professional and personal life. Her firm decision to leave work at 5:30 PM every day so she can enjoy dinner with her family is a testament to her understanding of the importance of setting boundaries. This practice, which she has followed since the early days of her career, is an affirmation of her deep-rooted values and highlights the significance of protecting personal time from professional encroachments.

But setting boundaries isn't merely about defining them; it also involves clearly communicating these limits to those around you. Sandberg's forthright disclosure about her work hours has set a precedent, proving that even high-powered executives can and should prioritize work-life balance. Her transparency has inspired many others to rethink their approach to their own work schedules, fostering a culture where personal time is respected.

However, establishing boundaries inevitably means learning to say 'no', a feat Sandberg has mastered well. Her steadfast commitment to her personal time meant respectfully declining late meetings or additional tasks that would bleed into her family time. It's this discernment, the ability to say no, that has been integral in preserving her energy, maintaining her focus, and ultimately, shielding her from the clutches of burnout.

To further illustrate her command over maintaining boundaries, Sandberg's strategic handling of workload is commendable. She excels in identifying and focusing on high-value activities, and effectively delegating tasks that others are equally capable of managing. This essential skill has ensured that she doesn't bite off more than she can chew, a trait that every entrepreneur can learn from to prevent burnout.

In an era where technology is omnipresent, Sandberg underscores the importance of carving out tech-free times to foster disconnection and focus. Despite leading one of the most prominent technology companies globally, she firmly believes in the restorative power of time spent away from screens.

Moreover, her interaction with multiple stakeholders exemplifies the maintenance of professional boundaries. She communicates clear expectations about her availability and responsiveness, setting a foundation for healthy and effective professional relationships without compromising her personal limits.

Even in the face of personal tragedy, Sandberg's resilience shone through as she reassessed and adjusted her boundaries. The loss of her husband in 2015 necessitated a reconsideration of her limits as she navigated her new circumstances as a single mother. This flexibility underscores the importance of reassessing and realigning boundaries in response to life's changes.

Sheryl Sandberg's story is a powerful reminder that setting boundaries and learning to say 'no' are not just options, but necessities for success and well-being. She's an embodiment of the concept that saying no is not a sign of incompetence or weakness, but an act of self-care. Her journey illuminates the path for all entrepreneurs striving to maintain their passion while preventing the debilitating effects of burnout. It teaches us that the art of setting boundaries is a continuous process, one that requires transparency, commitment, and the courage to prioritize ourselves.

A Personal Pause: Managing Boundaries in a Global Landscape

Navigating a nomadic lifestyle alongside a buzzing entrepreneurial journey is no easy feat, but with the right set of tools and a disciplined approach, it's not just possible but incredibly rewarding.

I rely heavily on **Calendly**, a fantastic tool integrated with all of my calendars. It's the linchpin in organizing my dispersed workflow, allowing me to manage time zones with teams distributed globally with a semblance of ease. It's not just a tool for me; it's a virtual assistant that handles the intricacies of scheduling, coordinating, and ensuring that I am exactly where I need to be at the right time.

Outsourcing tasks is a habit I've cultivated over the years, and it has been a lifesaver, albeit one that comes with its set of challenges. Time zones turn into a puzzle, a constant game of matching slots that fit everyone perfectly. It's here that setting strict boundaries comes into play, establishing firm lines that safeguard my personal time, even when dealing with collaborators from every corner of the globe.

But the nomadic lifestyle is more than a series of challenges; it's a path to freedom. It comes with a sense of liberation that is hard to describe. Yes, it requires an extensive amount of discipline and a firm grip on one's schedule, but the rewards are boundless. The freedom to work from anywhere, to find inspiration in the most unexpected places, and to set a personal schedule that respects both work commitments and the innate need for personal time and space.

Yet, this freedom isn't handed to you; it's earned through meticulous planning, respect for one's boundaries, and a nonnegotiable commitment to self-care. A nomadic entrepreneur is constantly drawing lines, setting boundaries that respect both the demands of work and the call of the open road, balancing the joy of discovery with the satisfaction of a job well done.

As we take a pause here, before embarking on the next leg of our entrepreneurial journey, I encourage you to reflect on the tools and strategies you employ in your daily life. Are they serving you well, aiding you in establishing and maintaining the boundaries that promote wellbeing and prevent burnout? Or is it time to reassess and recalibrate, to find new ways to protect your time and energy?

As we move forward, remember this: setting boundaries isn't about building walls; it's about carving out spaces for oneself in a world that constantly demands more. It's a respectful nod to our own needs, a way to safeguard our energy, and most importantly, it's the route to a fulfilling and sustainable entrepreneurial journey.

6

The Dance of Resilience: Mastering the Rhythms of Change and Adaptability

In this thrilling chapter, we embark on an exploration of resilience and adaptability, two invaluable companions in your entrepreneurial journey. The path to entrepreneurship is not a straight line; it's a journey etched with peaks, valleys, turns, and detours. By nurturing resilience and befriending adaptability, you can skillfully navigate these challenges, turning roadblocks into stepping stones on your path to success and keeping burnout at bay.

Demystifying Resilience: Resilience is your inner fuel, your capacity to bounce back stronger from adversity. Imagine a setback as a challenging mountain hike. Every stumble, every fall, is an opportunity to get up, dust yourself off, and learn how to step more surely. As you climb, you become better equipped for future hikes. As an entrepreneur, resilience is your capacity to get up after a stumble, use the experience to navigate better, and continue moving forward. Remember, resilience is not a passive trait; it's active and dynamic, transforming obstacles into stepping stones.

Forging Resilience: Resilience is like a blade, it is forged in fire and becomes stronger with each strike. Strive to see each setback as an opportunity to become stronger. Embrace failures as they provide you with a chance to test and improve your resilience. When you face a roadblock, instead of feeling defeated, ask yourself, 'What can I learn from this?' 'How can I use this to fuel my growth?' This will help you in transforming your resilience from a flickering flame to a roaring fire.

Cultivate a Growth Mindset: Adopt a growth mindset by seeking learning opportunities in each challenge. Whenever you encounter a hurdle, instead of thinking, "I can't do this," ask yourself, "What skills do I need to overcome this?" Commit to learning new skills, to continually growing and evolving. This approach not only helps you overcome immediate obstacles but also prepares you for future challenges.

Practice Self-Compassion: Think of how you would comfort a friend facing a similar challenge. What would you tell them? Likely, you'd provide words of encouragement, reassurance that it's okay to fail, and optimism for future success. Apply this same level of kindness and understanding to yourself. Remember, each stumble is a stepping stone towards success, and it's okay to give yourself some grace during the tough times.

Cultivate Emotional Intelligence: Emotional intelligence helps you maintain balance during the entrepreneurial rollercoaster ride. Start by reflecting on your emotions: why do you feel the way you do in certain situations? How do your emotions affect your decision-making? By understanding your emotional triggers, you can better manage your reactions, leading to healthier relationships and more thoughtful decisions.

Embracing Adaptability: Being adaptable is about being flexible with your plans while remaining focused on your ultimate goal. It's like using a GPS system: the destination is set, but the route can change based on traffic, road conditions, or new points of interest. Embrace this mindset in your business, being ready to adjust your strategies in response to market changes, customer feedback, or new insights, while staying committed to your core objectives.

Adopt a Learning Mindset: Continuous learning is crucial in the rapidly evolving entrepreneurial landscape. Attend industry seminars, sign up for relevant online courses, read widely, and stay curious. Foster a culture of learning within your organization by encouraging employees to upskill, share knowledge, and stay open to new ideas.

Welcome Change: Change, while sometimes unsettling, can be the catalyst for innovation. When market conditions shift or unexpected challenges arise, don't resist; instead, look for the opportunities these changes might present. It could be a chance to improve your product, explore a new market, or revamp your business model.

Foster a Culture of Adaptability: Promote flexibility in your organization by encouraging teams to brainstorm new ideas, experiment with different approaches, and learn from the outcomes. Recognize and reward innovative thinking and problem-solving. This helps create an environment where change is embraced, not feared, and adaptability becomes a key organizational strength.

Stay Agile: Agility means acting quickly and decisively in the face of new information or sudden changes. Implement systems that allow for rapid decision-making and encourage open communication to ensure everyone stays informed and ready to act. Regularly review and refine these systems for efficiency, ensuring your startup remains swift and nimble.

Develop a Growth Network: Networking is a powerful tool for growth. Regularly attend industry events, join online forums, and actively participate in relevant communities. Not only will you learn from the shared experiences and advice, but you can also form strategic partnerships, discover new business opportunities, and get insights into upcoming trends. Cultivate relationships with a diverse range of people - from peers to mentors, advisors, and even competitors.

Nurturing resilience and adaptability is a cornerstone in preventing burnout and maintaining your well-being as an entrepreneur. By forging resilience, you can bounce back from setbacks, extract wisdom from failures, and stay motivated when faced with challenges. By embracing adaptability, you can skillfully navigate the ever-shifting entrepreneurial landscape, seize opportunities, and stay ahead of the game.

Resilience and adaptability are not inborn traits that you either possess or lack. They are akin to skills that can be refined and nurtured over time. With practice, self-reflection, and an open heart to embrace change, you can fortify your ability to sail smoothly through the ebbs and flows of entrepreneurship, all while preserving your well-being.

Remember, resilience and adaptability are like two sides of the same coin, essential for thriving in the entrepreneurial world. They are the threads that weave the fabric of a successful entrepreneurial journey, helping you face any adversity and seize every opportunity that comes your way.

Case Study: Jack Ma's Dance with Resilience and Adaptability

Jack Ma, the charismatic co-founder and former executive chairman of Alibaba Group, has personified the art of resilience and adaptability throughout his entrepreneurial journey. From his early days as an English teacher to becoming the torchbearer of China's digital revolution, Ma's story is a testament to the power of tenacity, adaptability, and indomitable spirit.

Jack Ma's saga begins with rejection. He was turned down for numerous jobs, including at KFC and even after 10 attempts, he failed to secure a job with Harvard. But Ma did not surrender. Instead, he looked these failures straight in the eye and danced with them. His resilience - the sheer ability to bounce back and persevere, served as his sunrise after the darkest nights.

Part of Ma's resilience was his unwavering belief in himself and his vision. He fostered a growth mindset, viewing setbacks as teachers instead of tormentors. This growth-oriented perspective not only sustained him during challenging times but also sparked innovation and led to the birth of Alibaba. His trust in e-commerce, at a time when internet was still a novelty in China, was a sign of his problem-solving skills, which transformed a complex problem into a colossal opportunity.

However, the dance of resilience did not end there. Throughout Alibaba's growth, Ma faced several roadblocks - from financial crisis to stiff competition. Yet, each time, he found ways to overcome these obstacles by adopting a compassionate approach towards himself and his team. He frequently reminded himself and his team members that stumbling is a part of the journey and that it was crucial to be patient and supportive throughout the process.

Ma's ability to understand and manage emotions, both his own and his team's, was a testament to his high emotional intelligence. He prioritized fostering an emotionally aware and empathetic work culture, which aided in building strong relationships and navigating challenges effectively.

Resilience, however, was just one side of the coin. The other was adaptability. Jack Ma's dance with adaptability was equally captivating. From the outset, Ma embraced a learning mindset. He fostered an environment within Alibaba that encouraged continuous learning, innovation, and experimentation. He welcomed change and saw it as an opportunity to grow and evolve.

Ma also emphasized staying agile in the dynamic business landscape. He often spoke about responding swiftly to market changes and emphasized the importance of constant evolution to stay relevant. Alibaba's rapid adaptation to different industries, from retail and entertainment to cloud computing, is a testimony to Ma's vision of agility.

Furthermore, Ma understood the value of expanding his

network beyond his immediate industry. He made a conscious effort to expose himself and his team to fresh perspectives and ideas, ensuring Alibaba stayed at the forefront of innovation.

Jack Ma's journey illuminates the dance of resilience and adaptability in the entrepreneurial landscape. His ability to bounce back from setbacks, coupled with his readiness to adapt to change, prevented burnout and propelled him to unimaginable heights. His story serves as an inspiration to entrepreneurs worldwide, showing that with resilience and adaptability, one can navigate through the choppy seas of entrepreneurship, stay energized, and maintain a healthy balance between work and personal life.

A Personal Pause: The Unintended Entrepreneur's Path to Resilience

As we navigate through the realms of resilience and adaptability, I find it only right to pause and share a piece of my entrepreneurial journey with you. It began quite unexpectedly, when I ventured into establishing my first company, mypartner.com, a fusion of traditional matchmaking and online dating targeted specifically at gay men seeking long-term monogamous relationships. The inception of this company was not a calculated step but a response to a pressing need I identified while working towards my Ph.D. degree in Psychology after completing my Master's from San Francisco State University.

I never imagined that I would divert from my aspiration to become a psychologist and step into entrepreneurship. Yet, the path unraveled itself, inviting me to explore various avenues from launching a luxury men's skincare line after a stint with homemade colognes, to venturing into dog tech inspired by virtual fences.

While these projects bloomed into realities, there were hundreds of concepts that remained just that - concepts. But each venture, realized or not, added to my reservoir of experiences, constantly nurturing my resilience and adaptability, helping me dance gracefully with change, and challenging me to continually evolve.

These experiences taught me to embrace the ebbs and flows, to value the resilience built from failures, and to remain adaptable, always receptive to the opportunities each change presented. I invite you to carry this mindset as we venture deeper into the dynamics of entrepreneurship, where the only constant is change, and your ability to dance through it all is your greatest asset.

As we wrap up this enlightening exploration into the realms of resilience and adaptability, I hope that you find yourself better equipped, inspired, and eager to foster these vital traits within yourself and your venture. Much like my journey, which took unforeseen paths, leading to fruitful destinations, embracing change, and bouncing back with a stronger spirit is the essence of entrepreneurship.

As we step into the subsequent chapter, we turn our focus towards cultivating a positive and nurturing work culture. A space that recognizes and values each individual, promoting well-being and harmony.

We will delve deep into strategies to create an environment that not only focuses on business goals but also champions the well-being of every team member. It is here that we will uncover the transformative power of a healthy work culture, unveiling its potent role in not just preventing burnout but fostering a space where innovation, harmony, and well-being dance in beautiful synchrony, promising not just success, but a journey that is rich, fulfilling, and truly enjoyable.

Join me as we unravel the next layer in the intricate world of entrepreneurship, taking a step closer to building a startup that stands tall, rooted in resilience, blossoming with adaptability, and offering a nurturing haven for every individual that calls it home. Together, let us build not just successful ventures, but also thriving communities where every day is a testament to the harmonious dance of resilience and adaptability, fueling a journey marked by well-being and triumphant spirits.

7

Cultivating Harmony: Strategies for Fostering a Positive Work Culture

I magine yourself stepping into a place where every person is recognized for their unique strengths, where creativity is not just encouraged but celebrated. Picture an environment where communication is as transparent as crystal clear water, allowing trust to flow effortlessly. Envision a place where a sense of belonging blankets you, where achievements are recognized and appreciated with genuine gratitude. This utopia is not a figment of our wildest dreams but a tangible reality that entrepreneurs can cultivate within their startup - this is the realm of a positive work culture.

In the heart of the entrepreneurial hustle and bustle, work culture forms the very soul of your organization. It's not just about policies or procedures; it's about creating a nurturing environment that breathes life into your team's productivity, innovation, and overall job satisfaction. As we journey through Chapter 7 of our voyage into resilience and burnout prevention, let's delve into the nuances of nurturing a thriving work culture - an environment that brings out the best in your team while illuminating the path towards shared success.

Understanding Work Culture: Work culture is the invisible foundation upon which your startup is built. It's the unspoken language that echoes through the hallways, defining norms, shaping behaviors, and painting a picture of your organization's values and beliefs. A thriving, positive work culture is the backbone of entrepreneurial resilience - a sanctuary that bolsters well-being, stimulates creativity, and fuels collaborative endeavors.

Promoting Open Communication: In the vibrant tapestry of work culture, open communication threads itself as a vital strand. Encourage the exchange of ideas, constructive feedback, and expressions of thoughts within your startup. Like a river connecting diverse lands, open communication is the conduit that bridges gaps, fostering a haven of trust, respect, and shared understanding.

Empowering and Trusting Your Team: Your team is a constellation of unique stars, each shining with individual talents and capabilities. To foster a positive work culture, the power of empowerment and trust is paramount. Like the wind beneath the wings of a bird, entrust them with responsibilities and provide autonomy. This faith in their abilities unfurls a path of ownership, pride, and ultimate job satisfaction.

Encouraging Work-Life Balance: Amidst the bustling symphony of entrepreneurial ventures, the harmony of work-life balance mustn't be forgotten. Advocate for the establishment of clear boundaries between personal and professional lives. Your team are not just performers on your startup's stage; they are human beings who deserve rest, rejuvenation, and a fulfilling life outside work. Make a melody out of balance and prevent burnout from creeping into your harmonious composition.

Recognizing and Appreciating Achievements: In the orchestra of a positive work culture, each accomplishment, big or small, adds a unique note. Recognize these achievements and appreciate the dedication that led to them. Let your team members bask in the warmth of your gratitude, reinforcing their intrinsic motivation and enhancing job satisfaction.

Promoting Learning and Growth Opportunities: Your venture is a fertile ground for personal and professional growth. Nurture this soil with opportunities for learning, development, and mentorship. The growth of your team is a testament to your startup's success and a beacon of a positive work culture.

Creating a Supportive Environment: Weave the threads of support and collaboration into your work culture fabric. Like a safety net, a supportive environment cushions the falls and boosts the triumphs. By promoting a sense of camaraderie and collective responsibility, you foster a strong sense of belonging within your team.

Prioritizing Well-being Initiatives: Be the beacon that illuminates the importance of holistic health. Craft initiatives that advocate physical, mental, and emotional well-being, painting your startup as a sanctuary of health and balance. Embrace well-being not as an add-on but as an integral part of your work culture blueprint.

The Lighthouse of Entrepreneurship: An entrepreneur's journey isn't just about reaching the destination; it's about illuminating the path for others to follow. By fostering a positive work culture, you become a lighthouse guiding your team towards resilience, fulfillment, and a shared vision of success. Your team's collective well-being mirrors your startup's vibrancy and longevity. So, embrace your role as the architect of a thriving work culture and let your venture glow with positivity, respect, and shared growth.

Case Study: Satya Nadella's Transformation of Microsoft's Work Culture

In the realm of fostering a positive work culture, the remarkable journey of Satya Nadella, the CEO of Microsoft, stands out. Under his leadership, Microsoft experienced a cultural transformation that turned the tech giant into a haven of innovation, collaboration, and positivity.

Nadella stepped into the role of CEO in 2014 when Microsoft was going through a challenging phase. The culture was described as toxic, marked by fierce internal competition, leading to a stifling of innovation. Recognizing that the company's work culture was the invisible foundation upon which its future rested, Nadella set out to transform the corporate culture from a "know-it-all" to a "learn-it-all" mindset.

Promoting open communication was one of Nadella's primary initiatives. He believed that the transparent exchange of ideas and constructive feedback was crucial to Microsoft's success. He became an avid advocate for the freedom to express opinions, irrespective of hierarchy, promoting trust, mutual respect, and understanding.

Nadella put a substantial emphasis on empowering his team and trusting their potential. He encouraged risk-taking and celebrated learning from failures, fostering an atmosphere where each individual was given room to explore, grow, and shine. He demonstrated faith in his employees, providing them with autonomy and stimulating a sense of ownership that fueled job satisfaction.

Recognizing the importance of work-life balance, Nadella prioritized the well-being of his employees. He advocated for clear boundaries between personal and professional lives, championing initiatives that supported employees' holistic health and well-being.

An integral part of Nadella's positive work culture strategy was the recognition and appreciation of achievements. He ensured that employees felt seen and valued for their efforts, reinforcing their motivation and job satisfaction.

Nadella also prioritized learning and growth opportunities, transforming Microsoft into a vibrant platform for continuous development. He fostered an environment that encouraged learning, exploration, and innovation, with mentorship and development programs being vital elements.

Nadella also focused on creating a supportive environment within Microsoft. By encouraging collaboration and inclusivity, he nurtured a culture where everyone felt they belonged, boosting morale and fostering unity within the team.

Under Nadella's leadership, Microsoft saw a revival of its glory days. His strategies for fostering a positive work culture resulted in an increase in employee morale, collaboration, and overall productivity, leading to a remarkable growth in the company's market value.

Satya Nadella's transformative journey with Microsoft serves as an inspirational testament to the power of a positive work culture. His leadership underscores the importance of open communication, empowerment, work-life balance, recognition, learning opportunities, a supportive environment, and well-being initiatives in creating a thriving workplace. He has truly been a lighthouse guiding Microsoft towards resilience, fulfillment, and shared success, illuminating the path for other entrepreneurs to follow.

A Personal Pause: Harmonizing Productivity with a Four-Day Blueprint

As we journey through the intricacies of fostering a positive work culture, I find myself reflecting on my own practices as an entrepreneur. Implementing a work structure that echoes the sentiments of a 4-day work week, I have always reserved Fridays as a buffer day — a space for carrying over pending tasks. However, with diligent planning and execution, most of my tasks find their completion between Monday and Thursday.

I am a steadfast believer in the potential of a 4-day work week, a rhythm that doesn't compromise productivity but enhances it. It provides a sanctuary of balance, enabling me to dive deep into my entrepreneurial role while also fostering a culture of understanding and camaraderie with my team members. Yes, success, productivity, and a nurturing work environment are not only possible but can thrive in a 4-day work setup.

I share this to not only offer a glimpse into my journey but to showcase that as entrepreneurs, we have the power and the choice to craft a work culture that is both nurturing and exceptionally productive. It is a testimony to the fact that with harmony at the helm, a symphony of productivity, innovation, and joy is not just a dream but a tangible, achievable reality.

As we close this enlightening chapter on fostering a positive work culture — a haven of harmony, productivity, and mutual respect — we stand at the cusp of another crucial aspect of entrepreneurship: decision-making.

In our upcoming chapter we venture into the delicate dance of making decisions that not only steer the course of our startups but also deeply impact the lives intertwined with our entrepreneurial journey.

Decisions in the entrepreneurial world are a tightrope walk, a fine balance between logic and emotion, efficiency, and effectiveness. It is about navigating the tumultuous seas with a heart tuned to empathy and a mind sharpened for strategic insights.

Join me as we delve deeper into the art of decision-making, uncovering strategies to maintain a delicate equilibrium, fostering not just a successful startup but a journey marked with wisdom, empathy, and foresight.

Let's learn to walk this tightrope with agility, grace, and a heart brimming with resilience and understanding, forging a path that celebrates not just entrepreneurial acumen but the human spirit's indefatigable resilience and joy.

8

The Tightrope of Decision-Making: Striking the Balance Between Efficiency, Effectiveness, and Emotion

I n the fast-paced world of entrepreneurship, making hard decisions is an inevitable part of the journey. Determining when to reduce your workforce and when to scale up is a crucial aspect that often requires careful consideration. This chapter explores the key principles of efficiencies, effectiveness, and emotions in navigating these critical decisions.

Building Lean Teams: Every entrepreneur, at the height of their venture, stands on the precipice of significant choices. Like tightrope walkers, they're expected to balance, with grace and grit, the unpredictable winds of the business world. The first balance beam in this intricate dance of decision-making is building lean, efficient teams. Imagine a ballet ensemble, every dancer with a unique and irreplaceable role. Similarly, within the confines of a startup, each team member performs a delicate dance where every step counts. The secret to maintaining this dance's rhythm lies in precision - identifying the crux of your business objectives and aligning your team's talents to them. Foster a sense of ownership, instilling accountability and the drive for excellence. Parallelly, lay the groundwork for efficient processes, using technology as your choreographer, ensuring seamless, coordinated moves.

Effective Growth: As your venture dances to the beat of success, there comes a time to scale up. An invigorating, yet delicate phase. Like a musician preparing for a concert, the decision to scale up requires a careful reading of the audience - your market. Can your music resonate louder, reaching a larger crowd, while maintaining its soulful quality? Striking a balance between augmenting resources and retaining efficiencies is key. Prioritize the harmony of your ensemble, valuing cultural fit and shared company values. Just like an ever-evolving piece of music, keep revisiting your scaling strategy, adjusting your notes according to market rhythms.

Embracing Life Balance: However, while dancing to the tunes of efficiency and effectiveness, don't forget to step back and breathe. We are not just performers in this entrepreneurial ballet; we are human. And humans need a break. Here, we make an unconventional proposition: a 30-hour workweek. Rather than seeing it as a constraint, envision it as an opportunity to stimulate creativity and vitality within your team. Encourage smarter work, not harder. Value self-care, drawing the curtain on the unnecessary encore of overwork. This balance could be the secret to a vibrant, long-term performance.

Working Smarter, Not Harder: Working smarter, not harder is the new mantra. Like a maestro composing a symphony, an entrepreneur can weave a network of tools, technology, and strategic planning. Identify areas for automation, allow software to take the stage in organizing tasks, and encourage agile methodologies for flexibility. Prioritize and delegate tasks, letting each team member contribute their unique melody, freeing you to orchestrate the symphony.

Navigating Hard Decisions: Yet, amidst these decisions, lies another significant one - the role of emotions. Emotional intelligence is the unseen director guiding you through the twists and turns of the entrepreneurial narrative. In the face of hard decisions, like workforce reduction, it's the compass that enables you to tread the path of empathy and compassion. Open communication, transparency, and support during these transitions can transform a challenging scenario into an opportunity for growth and resilience. Cherishing the emotional well-being of your team cultivates a thriving ecosystem where they feel heard, valued, and supported. Remember, every member of your startup ensemble has a pivotal role, not just in performance, but in shaping the overall melody of your venture.

Case Study: Steve Jobs' Balancing Act of Decision-Making

When it comes to the challenging dance of decision-making, few can match the finesse and precision of Steve Jobs, the revolutionary co-founder of Apple Inc. His journey, peppered with dazzling highs and poignant lows, offers a masterclass in striking the balance between efficiency, effectiveness, and emotion.

In the early years of Apple, Jobs championed the concept of lean teams, each member assigned with a unique and vital role. He embodied precision in his approach, focusing on the essential aspects of his business and aligning his team to work towards those objectives. He encouraged each member to take ownership of their tasks and used technology as a tool to streamline the processes, ensuring a seamless and coordinated performance.

As Apple began to taste success, Jobs recognized the need for scaling, yet he understood that expansion should not compromise efficiency. He valued cultural fit and shared company values above all, ensuring the harmony of his team remained undisturbed. Jobs prioritized quality over quantity, a testament to his commitment to maintaining Apple's original charm and ethos even as it grew into a global phenomenon.

However, the charismatic entrepreneur also understood the importance of balance in life. While Jobs was known for his relentless work ethic, he often emphasized the need to work smarter, not harder. He encouraged his team to use technology and strategic planning to automate and delegate tasks, promoting agility and efficiency.

Despite his notorious reputation for being hard-nosed and demanding, Jobs was acutely aware of the role of emotions in decision-making. He used emotional intelligence to navigate tough decisions, particularly when it came to reducing his workforce during challenging times. Jobs communicated openly and honestly, ensuring his team felt valued and supported, even during the difficult periods.

Perhaps one of the most poignant examples of this was when Jobs was forced to leave Apple in 1985. His departure was emotionally charged, yet he managed to navigate this period with empathy and grace. He used this setback as a springboard for growth and resilience, ultimately returning to Apple years later to lead it to unprecedented success.

Jobs' ability to strike a balance between efficiency, effectiveness, and emotional intelligence formed the melody of his entrepreneurial journey. His leadership style and strategic decision-making helped shape Apple into the innovative powerhouse it is today. His story serves as a powerful reminder to entrepreneurs everywhere that success isn't simply about working harder or longer—it's about making informed, balanced decisions, working smarter, and understanding the emotional needs of your team. The applause of achievements and the hard decisions well-made, Steve Jobs left an enduring legacy that continues to resonate in the world of entrepreneurship.

A Personal Pause: Navigating the Delicate Dynamics of Team Harmony

In my journey, I have often found that walking the tightrope of decision-making becomes most personal and poignant when faced with the heartbreaking decision to part ways with a team member due to a mismatch in the team dynamics.

During my privileged time consulting with the founders of Good & Co, a pioneering psychometrics-based recruitment platform affectionately referred to as "LinkedIn meets eHarmony" or a "Quantified Glassdoor," I witnessed firsthand the power of a harmoniously matched team. The venture, which blossomed under the nurturing umbrella of StepStone and Axel Springer GmbH, stood as a testament to the fact that the success of a company is often woven from threads of well-matched team dynamics, defined not just by the competencies but the complementary energies and personalities.

However, harmony can sometimes be disrupted, leading to a discord in the symphonic venture. A misfit, much like a dissonant note in a melody, can reverberate beyond its immediate surroundings, affecting the morale and performance of the team at large. And this is especially true in the context of today's global, distributed teams, where culture and fit carry an even more significant weight in the scale of success.

I have always subscribed to a philosophy that may sound harsh but is grounded in a profound understanding of human dynamics: hire fast, fire faster. It is a principle built on the recognition that while someone might possess the skills to excel individually, a personality mismatch could potentially dampen the spirit and synergy of the team as a whole, eventually impeding everyone's path to success.

It is a tightrope walk, a delicate balance between giving an opportunity for growth and understanding when to make the tough call. Yet, at the heart of this philosophy lies a deep respect for the collective harmony, a commitment to fostering a space where every individual can flourish, creating a tapestry of success woven with threads of mutual respect, understanding, and shared objectives.

As we close this chapter, resonating with the reverberations of hard decisions and the symphonies of well-made choices, we set the stage for our next discussion - a deep dive into the alignment of work with one's deepest values and passions.

In the coming chapter, we journey into the heart of entrepreneurship, into the rich landscapes where work is not just a means to an end but a fulfilling pathway adorned with purpose, joy, and alignment with one's true calling. Prepare to immerse yourself in the dynamic interplay of values, passions, and entrepreneurship, as we unlock the secrets to a fulfilling entrepreneurial journey, where every step is a note in a melody sung from the heart, a dance performed with soulful grace. So, as we venture forth, let's carry with us the harmony we've nurtured thus far, ready to blend it with the vibrant rhythms of passion and purpose that await. Let's embrace the joy of crafting a business symphony that resonates with the deeper chords of our being, a venture that sings in harmony with our true selves.

9

The Pursuit of Fulfillment: Aligning Passion, Purpose, and Entrepreneurship

I magine a road not merely paved with the allure of financial gain but enriched with personal growth, meaning, and deep-seated satisfaction. As an entrepreneur, this path of fulfillment unfurls before you, interweaving your entrepreneurial pursuits with your core values, passions, and your innate desire to make a difference. It is on this journey that you'll uncover the true essence of entrepreneurship - a pursuit that transcends monetary success and is deeply embedded in the realms of purpose and fulfillment.

Embarking on a Journey of Fulfillment: As an entrepreneur, your venture provides an opportunity not just for financial growth, but also for personal development and purpose-driven achievement. Align your entrepreneurial pursuits with your core values and passions to enrich this journey. Keep a journal where you jot down what brings you joy and fulfillment, then consider how these elements can be integrated into your entrepreneurial activities.

Guided by Your Values: Your personal and business values act as your navigation system. To identify these, take some time to reflect on what truly matters to you and the impact you wish to make. Then ensure your startup's mission aligns with these values. This alignment can help steer your business decisions, creating a sense of authenticity and purpose in your entrepreneurial journey.

Crafting Your Personal Mission: A personal mission statement is a powerful tool that can guide you throughout your entrepreneurial voyage. To create yours, think about your ambitions and the impact you desire to have on the world. Write it down and revisit it, especially during challenging times, to remind yourself of your ultimate purpose.

Fueling Your Passion: Passion is a crucial driving force for any entrepreneur. Stay connected to what excites you by routinely engaging in activities that inspire and energize you. Regularly read, listen to podcasts, or engage in hobbies that keep your creative juices flowing. This will help you keep the spark alive and ensure that your entrepreneurial journey remains vibrant and fulfilling.

The Power of Connection: Building a network of supportive relationships is vital. Seek out mentors for guidance and peers for camaraderie. Join local business associations, online communities, or networking events to connect with others. Remember, these relationships can provide invaluable insight and support throughout your entrepreneurial journey.

Creating Ripples of Impact: Consider how your startup can make a positive difference. Can your product or service improve people's lives? Can you adopt more sustainable practices? Integrate these impactful elements into your business model and operations. This not only enhances your business's reputation but can also provide a deeper sense of fulfillment and purpose.

The Quest for Knowledge: Commit to continuous learning to grow both personally and professionally. Stay updated on industry trends, take relevant courses, and keep yourself open to new experiences. As you expand your knowledge and skills, you will find your entrepreneurial journey more empowering and fulfilling.

Celebrating the Journey: Recognition of your progress can fuel motivation. Celebrate your milestones, no matter how small, and practice gratitude for the lessons learned along the way. Keep a record of these successes and periodically review them. This will not only keep your spirits high but also provide a visual reminder of how far you've come.

Harmony in Work and Life: Balance is key. Rather than a rigid work-life separation, strive for an integrated and balanced lifestyle. This may involve setting boundaries, prioritizing self-care, and finding efficiencies in your work. As you achieve this balance, you'll likely find fulfillment permeating all areas of your life.

Case Study: Jamila Abass's Journey to Fulfillment

The entrepreneurial voyage of Jamila Abass, co-founder of M-Farm, illustrates the power of aligning passion, purpose, and entrepreneurship. As a technologist and an advocate for women in agriculture in Kenya, she has effectively combined her values, skills, and ambition to build a platform that empowers rural farmers.

Jamila's values revolve around the use of technology to alleviate social issues, particularly those faced by farmers in her native Kenya. These values were deeply ingrained in her vision for M-Farm, an agtech company that leverages mobile and web technology to connect small-scale farmers directly to markets. Her values guided M-Farm to become more than just a business; it became a movement towards agricultural equity and empowerment.

Crafting her personal mission, Jamila was driven by a fervor to democratize access to agricultural market information and eliminate exploitation of farmers by middlemen. M-Farm was the embodiment of this mission, using technology to provide up-to-date market information, linking farmers to buyers, and offering a platform for collective action.

Jamila's passion for tech and agriculture fuelled her venture. Even in challenging times, her dedication to M-Farm's mission and the farmers they serve never wavered. This unwavering passion ignited her entrepreneurial journey, turning it into a fulfilling adventure.

The power of connection was not lost on Jamila. She actively sought partnerships and collaborations to amplify M-Farm's impact. Her ability to form meaningful relationships with industry peers, government institutions, and international organizations was instrumental in M-Farm's success and scaling.

With M-Farm, Jamila created significant ripples of impact, serving over 20,000 farmers across Kenya, and improving their livelihoods. But she did not stop at economic impact; she also used her platform to advocate for gender equity in agriculture, empowering women farmers, and setting a strong example as a woman leader in tech.

Throughout her journey, Jamila embraced the quest for knowledge. From enrolling in coding boot camps to participating in entrepreneurial leadership programs, her pursuit of continuous learning underpinned her success and fulfillment as an entrepreneur.

Celebrating the journey, Jamila acknowledged each milestone, recognizing the progress made and lessons learned. In 2012, she was named a TED Fellow, and in 2013, Forbes listed her among 20 Youngest Power Women in Africa – affirmations of her hard work, progress, and the positive change she was driving.

Striking a harmony between her personal life and work, Jamila advocated for the importance of balance and well-being. She often emphasized the need for resilience and self-care in the grueling world of startups.

In essence, Jamila Abass's entrepreneurial journey embodies the pursuit of fulfillment. By aligning her passion, purpose, and entrepreneurial spirit, she has crafted a venture that transcends the traditional bounds of business, making significant strides in socio-economic development and leaving an indelible mark on Kenya's agricultural landscape.

A Personal Pause: From Creation to Fulfillment

Two decades of diving headfirst into the dynamic world of entrepreneurship, building startups from the ground up, and consulting for an array of promising ventures have equipped me with a rich tapestry of experiences. Today, as I pause and reflect, I realize that the heartbeat of my fulfillment resonates vibrantly in the arena of creation.

My hands have touched canvases blossoming into paintings and molded clay into structures, manifesting my artistic aspirations in the realm of hobbies. Yet, my true passion has always been in sculpting dreams into reality, in fostering visions until they stand tall, strong, and successful. I have cultivated joy through the metamorphosis of visions into tangible achievements, be it through rejuvenating the ugliest house on the block to stand as the most beautiful - a journey I have embarked upon 20 times over - or nurturing a startup to fruition.

This innermost passion for building and creating, for witnessing the transformation from the rudimentary to the remarkable, has been my North Star. It guided me as I sculpted visions into startups, dream into reality, and in that process, I discovered the potent brew of joy that comes from creating, from building, from taking something raw and forging it into something beautiful, resonant, and impactful.

I have found that, for me, fulfillment is a crafted sculpture, a house reborn, a startup soaring to heights previously unimaginable. It is the vibrant dance of vision and reality embracing in a waltz of creation, guided by hands that build with love, eyes that see with vision, and a heart pulsating with the joy of bringing dreams to life.

As we traverse this path together, mapping out the contours of a fulfilling entrepreneurial journey steeped in passion and purpose, we reach a pivotal junction. This junction heralds the approach to our final chapter, a chapter where we delve deep into the uncharted territories of entrepreneurial endeavors, exploring the intricate dance between passion and entrepreneurship.

In the forthcoming chapter, we will unravel the layers of fulfillment, uncovering the harmony that exists when passion meets purpose. It will be an exploration deep into the corridors of self, where you, as an entrepreneur, dance to the tunes of fulfillment, orchestrating a masterpiece that sings not only of financial success but of joy, growth, and deep-seated satisfaction.

As we stand on the cusp of this deep exploration, I invite you to accompany me with an open heart and a vibrant spirit, ready to embrace the possibilities that await when we align our innermost passions with our entrepreneurial spirit. Let us forge ahead with a spirit of adventure and the heart of a creator, ready to carve paths of fulfillment in the vibrant landscape of entrepreneurship, guided by the North Star of passion, purpose, and fulfillment that resonate so deeply within each one of us. Let us, together, set forth on this final leg of our journey, crafting narratives of success that are not just rich in financial gains but vibrant with purpose, joy, and personal fulfillment.

10

Onward and Upward: Essential Takeaways and Final Reflections for the Aspiring Entrepreneur

As we reach the end of our enlightening journey through the vibrant and ever-evolving landscape of entrepreneurship, it is a pivotal moment of reflection — a time to harvest the rich learnings and anticipate the promising paths that lie ahead. Throughout this journey, we have delved deep into the core of entrepreneurship, focusing not only on the passionate fire that drives it but also on the nurturing hands that sustain it.

Let us revisit the crucial revelations that we have unearthed:

Passion and Purpose as Twin Pillars: Passion and Purpose stand as the twin pillars of your entrepreneurial journey, acting as the guiding forces through the inevitable highs and lows. Yet, as steadfast as they are, they are not rigid constructs. As you grow and your business evolves, allow your passion and purpose to fluidly adapt, reflecting the learnings and experiences you accumulate along the way.

A savvy entrepreneur recognizes when to hold firm to their original vision and when to pivot, incorporating fresh perspectives and unexpected insights into a richer, more nuanced understanding of their venture's "why." Remember, the landscape of entrepreneurship is ever-changing; keeping an open mind and a flexible approach can foster a resilience grounded in reality, helping you navigate the path with wisdom and discernment.

Resilience, Your Mighty Shield: Like a seasoned sailor, you must build a robust shield of resilience, for it promises safety against the stormy weathers of doubt, fear, and exhaustion. Remember, this shield grows stronger with every challenge met and overcome, guarding not just your dream but your well-being.

Cultivating a Garden of Well-Being: Your entrepreneurial voyage is akin to nurturing a garden where each aspect of well-being — physical, mental, and emotional — needs tending to. Encourage a culture of balance and harmony, where burnout finds no ground to take root.

Leadership, A Beacon of Light: As you don the captain's hat, embody a leadership style rooted in empathy, understanding, and inclusivity. Be the beacon that guides and fosters a culture of resilience, shining brightly against the backdrop of the entrepreneurial cosmos, always steering clear of the burnout iceberg.

Collaborative Synergy: You are not alone in this voyage.

Build a network of fellow voyagers — mentors, advisors, and dreamers who sail similar seas. Share, learn, and grow together, creating a matrix of support that dissuades burnout and encourages resilience.

Customer-Centric Focus: Your venture's heartbeat is the customers. Engaging with them provides not just business insights but a fresh perspective and a renewed energy, fanning the flames of passion and creativity, keeping the fire alive and burning brightly.

Before we dive into our final case study, let's take a moment to reflect on what it truly means to "fuel your fire." It is a process that goes beyond just avoiding burnout. It is a conscious, continuous effort to nurture resilience, to tend to your inner flame, and to forge a path that is uniquely yours. It's about building a sanctuary of self-awareness, a space where you can rejuvenate, draw strength, and rise each day with renewed vigor, ready to face the entrepreneurial world with resilience and determination.

It is now time to explore a story that perfectly encapsulates this spirit of nurturing resilience and evading the claws of burnout. Let's delve into the extraordinary journey of Jeff Bezos, a man who managed to keep his inner flame burning bright, continuously fueling his fire to forge a path of legendary success.

Final Case Study: From Burnout to Billionaire: The Jeff Bezos Story of Resilience and Triumph

In the final case study of "Fueling the Fire: Nurturing Resilience and Preventing Burnout in Entrepreneurship," we encounter the remarkable story of Jeff Bezos, the visionary founder of Amazon. His journey not only epitomizes the entrepreneurial spirit but also serves as a beacon of inspiration for avoiding burnout and fostering a sustainable path to success.

Jeff Bezos's entrepreneurial voyage began in 1994 when he founded Amazon as an online bookstore. With a relentless pursuit of customer-centric innovation, he transformed Amazon into the e-commerce giant it is today, revolutionizing the retail industry. Along the way, Bezos faced numerous challenges and setbacks, but his unwavering resilience and commitment to his long-term vision propelled him forward.

As the success of Amazon grew, Bezos recognized the importance of maintaining balance and well-being amidst the demands of entrepreneurship. He understood that the path to sustainable success required strategic choices and self-care practices to prevent burnout. Bezos implemented several strategies to nurture his well-being and protect his mental and physical health.

First and foremost, Bezos prioritized time for reflection and self-renewal. He recognized the value of stepping back from the day-to-day operations and creating space for strategic thinking, innovation, and personal growth. By carving out dedicated periods for contemplation, Bezos ensured that he remained connected to his vision and purpose, while also finding inspiration to navigate challenges with clarity.

Additionally, Bezos embraced a growth mindset and a willingness to delegate and empower his team. He understood that he couldn't do it all alone and that relying on a capable and motivated team was essential for scaling his venture. By trusting his team members and empowering them to make decisions, Bezos not only alleviated the burden on himself but also fostered a culture of collaboration and shared responsibility.

Recognizing the importance of physical well-being, Bezos incorporated regular exercise into his routine. Whether it was morning workouts or engaging in outdoor activities, he understood that a healthy body was the foundation for a healthy mind and sustained energy levels. By investing in his physical health, Bezos fortified his ability to navigate the demanding landscape of entrepreneurship with vitality and focus.

Furthermore, Bezos cultivated a supportive network of mentors and advisors. He sought guidance from experienced entrepreneurs and industry experts who could provide insights, support, and wisdom. By surrounding himself with a trusted circle of individuals who understood the unique challenges of entrepreneurship, Bezos not only received valuable advice but also developed a strong support system to lean on during challenging times.

Throughout his journey, Bezos emphasized the importance of maintaining a long-term perspective and avoiding the trap of short-term burnout. He understood that sustainable success was not measured solely by immediate gains but by the ability to endure and thrive in the face of adversity. By staying focused on his long-term vision and remaining resilient, Bezos exemplified the art of preventing burnout and achieving enduring success.

Jeff Bezos didn't just prioritize personal well-being and resilience; he instilled a similar approach in his team, fostering a culture that emphasized innovation and a relentless focus on the customer — the true north of Amazon's compass. By encouraging his team members to take ownership, think big, and obsess over customers, Bezos promoted an environment where creative solutions were nurtured and celebrated.

In this nurturing space, team members felt empowered to innovate, constantly pushing boundaries to better serve customers, all while supporting each other's well-being. This approach cultivated resilience at both an individual and organizational level, creating a cycle of positive reinforcement where well-being and success were intrinsically linked, a testament to the far-reaching benefits of nurturing a resilient, customer-centric ethos.

A Personal Pause: Nurturing Resilience in the Entrepreneurial Journey

As I stand amidst the whirling dynamics of entrepreneurship, a journey woven with dreams, aspirations, and countless moments of tenacity, I am compelled to share a seminal chapter from the saga, a period marked with both trials and tribulations.

In the early stages of my entrepreneurial journey, there came a time many founders dread: the turbulent waters of fundraising. It was a relentless whirlpool of pitching and networking, a daily grind to showcase our vision's viability to potential investors. This period, fraught with a rollercoaster of emotions, swung between peaks of hope and valleys of rejection.

The flames of my passion and purpose seemed to waver, threatened incessantly by gusts of uncertainty and exhaustion. Yet, in the face of adversity, I forged a sanctuary within, a space of solitude where I could reconnect with my venture's essence, rekindling the initial sparks that ignited this ambitious journey.

I remember distinctly a day laden with despair, feeling the weight of repeated no's. I found myself alone in my small home office, seemingly engulfed by the amplifying echo of rejection, a sound that threatened to drown my spirit. But amidst this chaos, I chose to stand still, to take a personal pause and distance myself from the all-consuming task of fundraising.

This pause became a wellspring of rejuvenation, a moment of reflection where I could touch base with the unwavering belief that fueled our mission from the inception. I allowed myself to navigate through the narratives, not as rehearsed pitches but as heartfelt stories brimming with hope, potential, and a vision for a better future.

As I nurtured self-compassion and fostered a grounded determination, I embarked on a journey inward, rediscovering the dreams and visions that lay at the heart of our venture. The authentic reconnection with the spirit of our mission brought forth a resurgence of genuine enthusiasm and a deeper conviction in the path we were forging.

Returning to the fundraising arena with a rejuvenated spirit, a shift had occurred. The pitches transformed into genuine narratives, a vivid painting of dreams and visions shared with sincerity and newfound resilience. This transformation was palpable, resonating with potential investors who could sense the deep-seated belief and genuine passion driving our venture.

This introspective journey illuminated the indispensable value of balanced growth and self-care, highlighting the virtues of vulnerability and humility. The path unfurled with a richer understanding, revealing that success is indeed a collaborative endeavor, a harmonious blend of individual tenacity and collective synergy.

It was during these moments I embraced the ebb and flow

of the entrepreneurial tide, learning to lean on the supportive shoulders of a team unified in vision and purpose, nurturing relationships that fed my soul and fortified my resolve.

As I look back, I treasure this chapter as a testament to the transformative power of a personal pause, a beacon illustrating the nurturing spirit of resilience born from shared experiences and mutual growth.

As we stand on the cusp of new beginnings, let us carry forward this nurturing spirit, holding close the lessons ingrained in our journey. Let us forge paths of unparalleled success and fulfillment, grounded in well-being, balance, and a vibrant energy, united in purpose and passion, always ready to embrace both challenges and triumphs with a heart brimming with hope. Let us remain buoyed by the collective dreams and aspirations of a community united in purpose and passion, marching forward with harmonious growth at the helm, on a path etched with joy, purpose, and the unyielding belief in creating something truly magnificent.

As we close this chapter, remember that the spirited landscape of entrepreneurship beckons, laden with opportunities hidden in challenges, successes arising from failures, and learning carved from experiences.

Jeff Bezos's journey serves as a testament to the power of resilience, balanced well-being, and a fervent yet grounded ambition. His story vividly illustrates the rich tapestry that awaits when you walk a sustainable path to success, striking a balance between unrestrained passion and a nurturing environment that fosters well-being. However, it is pivotal to also address the substantial criticism and controversy that has surrounded Bezos's tenure, notably concerning workplace conditions and labor practices at Amazon. While he has indeed reached pinnacles of success and innovation, the journey has been marred by allegations of harsh working conditions and a high-pressure work environment. This underscores the necessity for aspiring entrepreneurs to foster a culture of empathy and well-being, not just for oneself but for every individual contributing to a venture's growth. Navigating such complexities with a conscientious approach will be the hallmark of a leadership style that truly stands the test of time.

Brave entrepreneurs, you are on the verge of stepping into an exhilarating path guided by resilience as your north star. As you forge your unique path of significance, remember to carry wisdom in one hand and passion in the other, constantly fueling the internal fire that drives you while guarding fiercely against burnout.

May your voyage be fulfilling, your spirit ever vibrant, and your resilience unyielding. Keep nurturing that intrinsic fire with knowledge and an unwavering heart, refusing to succumb to burnout.

Bon voyage, as you embark on this path of nurtured re-silience, armed with the distilled wisdom encapsulated in these pages. May you carve out a journey of triumph, leaving a unique imprint on the world and fueling the immortal fire of entrepreneurship.

-THE END-

The Ask

Dear Resilient Reader,

Did I fan the flames of your entrepreneurial spirit? If this book added some kindling to your fire, why not share the warmth with a review on Amazon?

If you think it deserves a five-alarm rating, fantastic! But remember, your honest thoughts are the hottest commodity.

Ready to fuel more fires? Explore my **Amazon author's page** (https://www.amazon.com/author/patrickhperrine) to stoke your knowledge even further.

Let's keep the entrepreneurial fires burning brightly, one candid review at a time.

Warm Regards,
Patrick

About the Author

Patrick H. Perrine is a trailblazing author, mentor, and seasoned entrepreneur with a spirit that exemplifies the essence of entrepreneurship. From his humble beginnings as a paperboy in Minnesota to his emergence as a globally recognized industry leader, his journey epitomizes resilience and determination.

Fueled by an insatiable thirst for knowledge, Patrick opted for university over his senior high school year, setting the stage for his relentless pursuit of personal growth. His tenure with UpStart, an organization championing educational opportunities for first-generation Americans, ignited his lifelong commitment to empowering others, extending beyond business and into his early philanthropic endeavors.

In his twenties, Patrick served as a Founding Board member for The Point Foundation, the largest LGBTQ scholarship foundation today. His dedication to fostering inclusivity and aiding LGBTQ students in higher education continues to positively impact hundreds of lives.

Patrick's entrepreneurial journey took flight with myPartner.com, an online dating service that addressed a critical gap in the market. Recognized as one of the "Best Matchmakers" and "Most Innovative Online Dating Sites" by the iDate Industry, the venture earned a Certificate of Recognition issued by California Legislature Assemblyman Mark Leno. This marked Patrick's first step in a journey filled with identifying unique opportunities and delivering transformative solutions across industries from skincare to dog tech.

Despite the hurdles encountered, Patrick's determination only amplified. His passion for nurturing startups led him to establish Rincon Hill Advisors. During this period, he served as a Steering Committee member for StartOut, a leading nonprofit fostering queer entrepreneurship, and consulted with Fortune 500 companies like Berkshire Hathaway and Intuit.

Adding to his achievements as an entrepreneur, Patrick became an angel investor. His foresight led him to invest in promising startups like MisterB&B, the world's largest gay hotelier, and Roadster, the leading commerce platform for car buying. His dog tech venture, too, gained recognition, leading to his selection as a NGLCC Pitch Finalist and participant in the Seamless IoT Accelerator, earning a $100,000 investment offer as a program graduate.

Most recently, Patrick served as an Entrepreneur in Residence (EiR) with 500 StartUps, an organization committed to uplifting global economies through entrepreneurship. This role solidified his dedication to guiding and uplifting aspiring entrepreneurs.

With a total of ten books and counting to his credit, including recent works "Fail Fast, Recover Faster", "Ignite your Dream", and "Fueling the Fire", Patrick continues to share his journey and insights. His writing reflects his unwavering commitment to guiding entrepreneurs through their unique journeys.

Patrick H. Perrine is more than a summary of his accomplishments. He stands as a testament to the power of determination, innovation, and a generous spirit. His contributions have been acknowledged in global press publications such as Forbes, Advocate, and Mirror, but his most profound impact lies in the lives of the entrepreneurs he's guided, inspired, and empowered. As he continues sharing his wisdom in the 10 volume series "Be A Unicorn: The New Entrepreneur's Ultimate Guide to Success", Patrick personifies the quintessential entrepreneurial journey—one of resilience, innovation, and the relentless pursuit of personal growth.

Subscribe to my newsletter:

✉ https://www.patrickperrine.com

Also by Patrick H. Perrine

Your next adventure in entrepreneurship awaits! Choose your guidebook on Amazon or **www.PatrickPerrine.com/books**, and ignite the spark that takes your venture to new heights. The future is yours to shape!

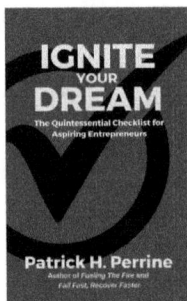

Ignite your Dream: The Quintessential Checklist for Aspiring Entrepreneurs
Ignite your Dream: The Quintessential Checklist for Aspiring Entrepreneurs" by Patrick H. Perrine is an immersive guide lighting the path towards entrepreneurial success. This power-packed handbook propels you from dreaming to achieving with a carefully curated 100-step map. Dive into real-life entrepreneur stories, extract wisdom, and utilize actionable checklists. This book transcends theoretical guidelines, providing a mentorship experience designed to turn dreams into reality. Ready to kindle your entrepreneurial spirit? "Ignite your Dream" is your step forward towards unlocking potential and achieving success in the exciting world of entrepreneurship.

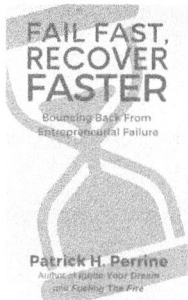

Fail Fast, Recover Faster: Bouncing Back From Entrepreneurial Failure

Embrace failure and bounce back stronger with "Fail Fast, Recover Faster: Bouncing Back From Entrepreneurial Failure". It's your guidebook through the tumultuous journey of entrepreneurship, celebrating stumbles as stepping stones towards success. Dive into compelling tales of triumphant entrepreneurs, learn how to pivot rapidly, manage fallout, and convert setbacks into launchpads. Discover strategies for repairing financial, relationship, and reputation damage, and see your failures as badges of resilience. This transformative book readies you to rebound from failure swiftly, turning your setbacks into your next entrepreneurial triumph. With "Fail Fast, Recover Faster", you're poised to harness your own unicorn moment and turn failure into a launching pad for success.

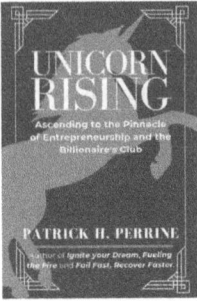

COMING SOON: Unicorn Rising: Ascending to the Pinnacle of Entrepreneurship and the Billionaire's Club

Fueled by entrepreneurial dreams and the allure of the Unicorn Club? Patrick H. Perrine is your guide, offering an unparalleled roadmap set to be every entrepreneur's playbook.

"Unicorn Rising" is more than a path to towering valuations; it's a compass to innovation, transformative leadership, and sustainable triumph. Dive into leadership's intricacies, the pulse of emerging tech, financial stewardship, and the essence of high-impact entrepreneurship.

However, this isn't a one-size-fits-all roadmap. While Patrick offers foundational wisdom and actionable tools, he accentuates the bespoke nature of each startup's odyssey. Whether you're an entrepreneurial novice or a battle-hardened veteran seeking to recalibrate strategies, this series becomes your beacon.

Embark, defy conventions, and with "Unicorn Rising," elevate to unparalleled entrepreneurial echelons.

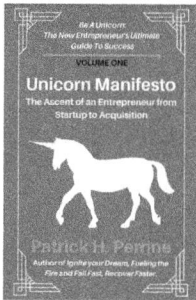

COMING SOON: Be A Unicorn: The New Entrepreneur's Ultimate Guide To Success

The comprehensive 10-volume series designed to navigate the thrilling terrain of entrepreneurship. Covering the crucial aspects of startup life, the series provides in-depth insights into business strategy, leadership, risk management, innovation, marketing, personal development, finance, technology, and social entrepreneurship. Each volume is a deep dive into a specific topic, packed with actionable strategies, real-life case studies, and practical advice. Whether it's developing robust business models, fostering creativity, mastering sales techniques, setting personal goals, or creating a social impact, this series arms entrepreneurs with the tools needed to succeed in today's dynamic business landscape. "Be A Unicorn" is your roadmap to entrepreneurial success, guiding you from startup ideation to long-term triumph. Let's turn your entrepreneurial dreams into reality, one book at a time.